Studies and Melodious Etudes for Oboe

by

Blaine Edlefsen
in collaboration with
Fred Weber

To The Teacher

"Studies And Melodious Etudes", Part I, is a supplementary technic book of the Belwin "STUDENT INSTRUMENTAL COURSE". Although planned as a companion and correlating book to the method book, "The Oboe Student", it can also be used effectively with most elementary oboe instruction books. It provides for extended and additional treatment in technical areas, which are limited in the basic method because of lack of space. Emphasis is on developing musicianship through scales, warm-ups and technical drills, musicianship studies and interesting melody-like etudes.

The Belwin "STUDENT INSTRUMENTAL COURSE" - A course for individual and class instruction of LIKE instruments, at three levels, for all band instruments.

EACH BOOK IS COMPLETE IN ITSELF BUT ALL BOOKS ARE CORRELATED WITH EACH OTHER

METHOD

The Oboe Student
For individual
or
Oboe Class
instruction.

ALTHOUGH EACH BOOK CAN BE USED SEPARATELY, IDEALLY, ALL SUPPLEMENTARY BOOKS SHOULD BE USED AS COMPANION BOOKS WITH THE METHOD

STUDIES AND MELODIOUS ETUDES

Supplementary scales, warm-up and technical drills, musicianship studies and melody-like studies.

TUNES FOR TECHNIC

Technical type melodies, variations, and "famous passages" from musical literature --- for the development of technical dexterity.

THE OBOE SOLOIST

Interesting and playable graded easy solo arrangements of famous and well-liked melodies.
Easy piano accompaniments.

How To Read The Chart

● — Indicates hole closed,
or keys to be pressed.

○ — Indicates hole open.

■ When two ways to finger a note are given, the first way is the one most often used. The second fingering is used in special situations.

■ When two notes are given together (F# and G♭ for example), they sound the same pitch and are, of course, fingered the same way.

In order to make this chart as easy to understand as possible, only those fingerings necessary to play this method book are given.

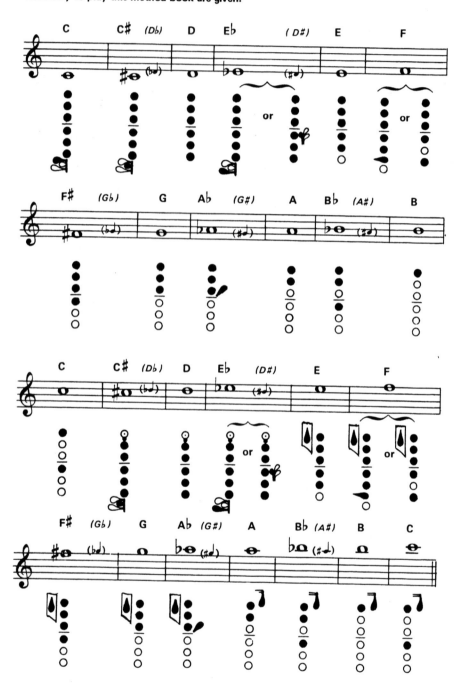

1st Octave Key

2nd Octave Key

C - Pad Spatula

Half Hole

C - D Trill

B - C# Trill

Left G#

Low B

G# - A Trill or A♭ -B♭ Trill

Low B♭

Right G#

Left E♭

C - D Trill

Right F

Extra Low C

Low C

Low C#

Right E♭

The Studies and Etudes on this page correlate approximately with page 6, Lesson 3, of the oboe method book, "The Oboe Student." The correlation is continued throughout the books.

Also F#— a sharp carries throughout the measure.

Etude No. 1

Etude No. 2

APR 14

① Hold oboe down
② Keep on lower lip when you exhale
③ keep the lower lip tucked
④ corners in - ⑤ hold tongue forward when slurring + tonguing

Centered round tone

Repeat each section until the intervals are clean and the rhythm is precise.

Slur two ways.

(1) Slur all. (2) Tongue all. (3) Slur as written.

(1) Slur all. (2) Tongue all. (3) Slur as written.

Etude No. 3

-2nd time-

Etude No. 4

Apr 28

Play all F♮'s on this page with the right hand f key.

Repeat each measure until clean.

Slur as marked, then tongue.

Work for speed and rhythmic accuracy.

Etude No. 5

Etude No. 6

6

May 5

Etude No. 7

Etude No. 8

NOTE: For this page and the remainder of this book, play the f's marked F with the forked fingering and those marked R with the right hand key. If your oboe has a left hand f key, practice all the passages using that key for those f's marked F whenever possible, and in addition, you must practice using the forked f fingerings.

Forked-F Studies

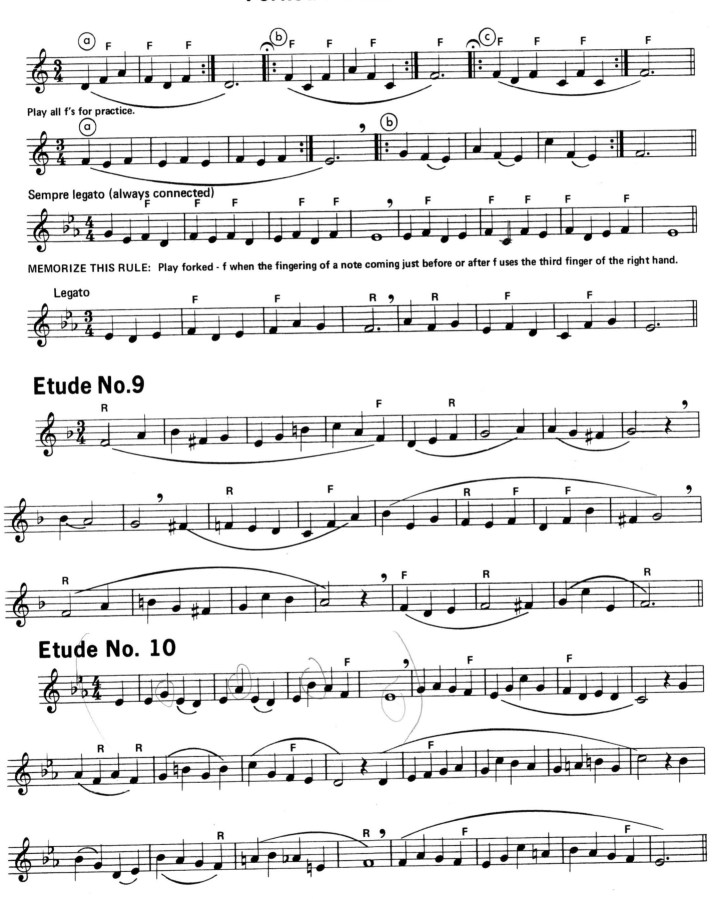

Play all f's for practice.

Sempre legato (always connected)

MEMORIZE THIS RULE: Play forked - f when the fingering of a note coming just before or after f uses the third finger of the right hand.

Legato

Etude No. 9

Etude No. 10

MAY19

Half Hole Studies

- Round mouth
- high speed if air
- feel the tip of r...
  wi
  tongue

Etude No. 11

Half Hole Etude

Etude No. 12

Half Hole Etude

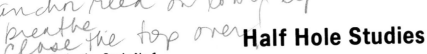

Half Hole Studies

Octave Reduction Study No. 1
First learn the exercises legato, then practice tonguing them.

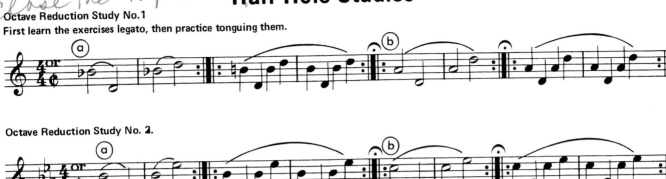

Octave Reduction Study No. 2.

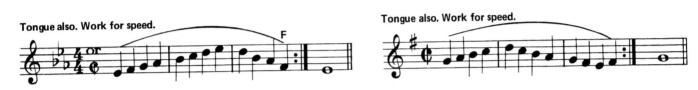

Tongue also. Work for speed.   **Tongue also. Work for speed.**

Etude No. 13

Half Hole Etude

From this point on, fewer right hand f's and forked f's will be marked.

Etude No. 14

Half Hole Etude

B.I.C.122

Hold the tones long and steady.

Use the first octave key (1 OK) with these notes. DO NOT USE the half hole.

On wide ascending intervals, roll the reed farther into the mouth. Roll the reed out for the descending ones. DO NOT let the reed slip in and out; we simply roll it. Do not drop the jaw.

Octave Reduction Study
Slur first, then tongue.

Etude No. 15
First Octave Key Etude

Etude No. 16
First Octave Key Etude

Studies Combining the First Octave Key and Half Hole Movements.

Slur as marked, then tongue.

G Major Scale — Stepwise

F Major Scale — Stepwise

Etude No. 17

Etude No. 18

Playing The Right Hand E♭-D♯ Key

Etude No. 19
Key of B♭ Major

Etude No. 20
Key of G Minor

Slur then tongue.

D Major Scales - Stepwise and in thirds.
Slur two ways, then tongue all.

Chromatic Scale Studies
Tongue also

Half Hole (hh)   1st Octave Key (1 OK)

Play both octaves.

Etude No. 21
Chromatic March

Etude No. 22

Eighth Notes

Play precisely in rhythm with quick finger movements.

Play 3 times (3x)

Slur each measure, then play as marked. Last of all, tongue each note.

Play each section several times for speed, rhythmic accuracy, and neatness.

Etude No. 23

Etude No. 24

Controlling Loudness For More Expressive Playing

Etude No. 25

Etude No. 26

Etude No. 27

Moderately

Etude No. 28

1st time
2nd time

Half Hole review
Repeat each exercise several times.

1st Octave Key Review

Combining The Half Hole And First Octave Key Movements: A Review.

Etude No. 29
Half hole and first octave key movements.

Etude No. 30

Left Hand A♭ Study

Slur two ways, then tongue all.

Half Hole To A♭ Study

Slur two ways, then tongue all.

Chromatic Study

Tongue also

Left Hand Study

Etude No. 31

Etude In E♭ Major

Etude No. 32

First Etude In C Minor

Staccato

Etude No. 33

Moderately fast

Etude No. 34

Staccato Etude In E Minor

Fast

(You must tongue each note on the repeat.)

Very slow

NOTE:

means gradually softer (decrescendo or diminuendo)

means start loudly, then decrease gradually to soft.

Very slow (You must tongue each note on the repeat.)

STUDY PROCEDURE: (1) Play all f's forked. (2) Practice lower octave first. (3) Play legato always.

Staccato Study

Fast

Etude No. 35

Sempre piano

Etude No. 36

B.I.C.122

means crescendo (cresc.) — play gradually louder.

USING THE SECOND OCTAVE KEY
Octave Reduction Studies

DOTTED QUARTER NOTES

Etude No. 37

Etude No. 38

Fine

D. C. al Fine

Etude No. 39

Etude No. 40

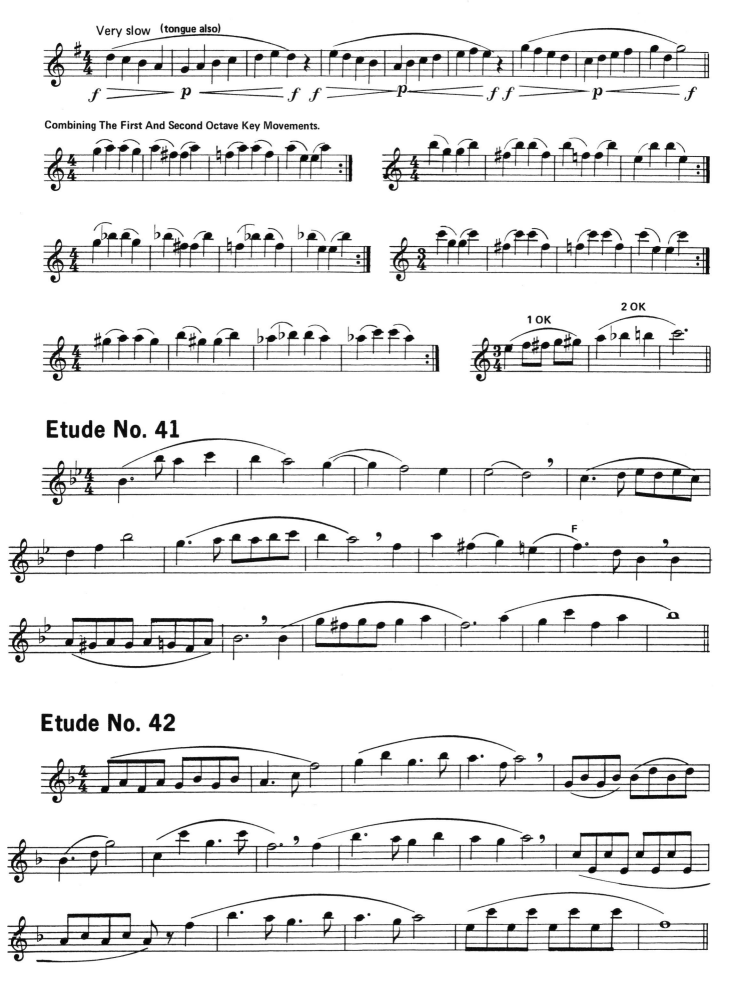

Etude No. 41

Etude No. 42

F Major Scale

Bb Major Scale

C Major Scale

A Major Scale

Combining The First And Second Octave Key Movements

* Etude No. 43

Etude No. 44

Fine

D. C. al Fine

Half Hole Movement Review

Second Octave Key Movement Review

Changing Registers on the Oboe

Etude No. 45

Etude No. 46

Apply these patterns to the scales above.

Combining The Half Hole And Second Octave Key Movements.

Etude No. 47

Etude No. 48

Etude No. 49

Etude No. 50

(Use left E♭ – D♯ Key.)

Left Hand E♭–D♯ Key Review

Play the low C's with the flat part of the finger.

Arpeggios

Slur all first, then tongue all.

Etude No. 51

(Play all eighth notes slurred, then staccato, then as marked.)

NOTE: After you have learned Etude No. 51 well, practice it thoroughly one octave higher.

Etude No. 52

Accents

Play measures 1, 2, and 3 alike.

Sixteenth Notes

Apply this pattern to the following notes.

To accent, play louder during the first part of the tone than during the last part. Accented tones are louder than unaccented ones.

Passages to Left Hand E♭- D♯ Half Hole.
Play two ways. Use the lowest octave note first.

Slur two ways.

Etude No. 53

Etude No. 54

simile

B.I.C.122

Accents And Staccato

Chromatic Scale

Slur two ways after studying it legato.

PATTERN: ① ② ③

Apply these rhythms to each scale above.

Etude No. 55

Etude No. 56

Combining 1st and 2nd Octave Key Movements.

Passages to the Half Hole.

Combining Half Hole and 1st Octave Key Movements.

Combining Half Hole and 2nd Octave Key Movement

(Use right and left Eb's.)

(Use right and left Eb's)

Study legato first, then slur two ways.

Etude No. 57

Very legato

Etude No. 58

Very slow

Play first slurred, then all staccato, then as marked.

simile

Play 3 ways (1) all slurred, (2) all staccato, (3) as marked.

Etude No. 59

(Use right hand F Key throughout.)

Etude No. 60